The RENAISSANCE

Revised and Updated

JANE SHUTER

Heinemann Library
Chicago, Illinois

© 1998, 2007 Heinemann Library
a division of Reed Elsevier Inc.
Chicago, Illinois

Customer Service 888-454-2279
Visit our website at www.heinemannraintree.com

Designed by Richard Parker and Q2A Solutions
Printed in China by WKT Company Ltd

11 10 09 08 07
10 9 8 7 6 5 4 3 2 1

New edition ISBNs: 1-403-48814-2 (hardcover)
                             1-403-48821-5 (paperback)
13 digit ISBNs: 978-1-403-48814-5 (hardcover)
                          978-1-403-48821-3 (paperback)

The Library of Congress has cataloged the first edition as follows:
Shuter, Jane.
   The Renaissance / Jane Shuter.
   p.   em. — (History opens windows)
   Summary: An introduction to the various elements of Renaissance life, including religion, trade, education, food, and clothes.
   ISBN 1-57572-887-7 (lib. bdg.)
   1. Includes bibliographical references and index. 2. Renaissance-Juvenile literature.
   3.Civilization, Medieval—Juvenile literature. 4. Civilization, Modern—Juvenile literature.
   5. Europe—History—476—1492—Juvenile literature.
   6. Europe—History—1492—1648—Juvenile literature. [1. Renaissance.] I. Title. II. Series.
   D228.S54   1999
   940.2'1—dc21
                                99-11817
                                  CIP
                                  AC

Acknowledgments
The publisher would like to thank the following for permission to reproduce photographs:
Alamy, p. **10**; Bridgeman Art Library/Palazzo Medici-Riccardi, p. **7**; Bridgeman Art Library/Museo di Firenze Com'era, p. **6**; Scala/S. Trinita, Firenze, p. **8**; Bodleian Library, p. **12**; Bridgeman Art Library/British Museum, p. **14**; British Museum, p. **16**; Bridgeman Art Library/Duomo, Florence, p. **17**; Bridgeman Art Library/Palazzo Ducale, Mantua, p. **18**; Bridgeman Art Library/Biblioteca Trivulzana, Milan, p. **20**; Bridgeman Art Library/Giraudon, p. **21**; Bridgeman Art Library/Christie's, London, p. **21**; Bridgeman Art Library, p. **23**; Scala/Museo Poldi Pezzoli, p. **24**; Bridgeman Art Library/Kunsthistorisches Museum, Vienna, p. **25**; Bridgeman Art Library/Private Collection, p. **26**; Bridgeman Art Library/British Library, p. **27**; Wellcome Institute Library, London, p. **29**; Bridgeman Art Library/Fratelli Fabri, Milan, p. **29**.
Illustrations: Eileen Mueller Neill, p. **4**; Bill Le Fever, p. **9, 11, 25**; James Field, p. **13, 15**; Tony Randall, p. **28**; Finbarr O'Connor, p. **30**.

Cover photograph reproduced with permission of AKG-Images / Erich Lessing

Contents

Some words are shown in bold, **like this**.
You can find out what they mean by looking in the glossary.

Introduction

This map shows the Italian city-states in about 1450. City-states fought each other and borders kept shifting.

Map labels:
Turin
Saluzzo
Tandon
Milan
Genoa
Venice
Mantua
Ferrara
Ravenda
Malaspina
Modena
Lucca
Florence
Sienna
Turin
The Papal States
Ruled by Holy Roman Empire
Ruled by Genoa
Rome
Naples
Ruled by Aragon
Ruled by Aragon
Ruled by Aragon
MEDITERRANEAN SEA

1410: Jan Van Eyck discovers oil paints

1420: Palazzo built in Venice decorated with gold stones

1496: Spain and Portugal get permission from the Pope to divide the New World between themselves

1400   **1450**   **1500**

1405-52 huge bronze doors
1410-36 Brunelleschi's dome
Major Rebuilding of Florence Cathedral

1406: interest in Greek and Roman writings begins when Ptolemy's *Geography* rediscovered

1440: printing press developed using movable metal letters

1492: explorer Christopher Columbus reaches the West Indies. Martin Behain makes first globe map of the world

Renaissance means "rebirth." It was a time in Europe when many people were fascinated by the ancient Greeks and Romans. People wanted to bring the ancient world back to life—to be "reborn."

As well as rediscovering old ideas, it was also a time for making new discoveries. One important discovery was the **printing press**. Because of the printing press, many more people could afford books, and many more people learned to read.

The Renaissance began in Italy and spread over Europe, along trading routes. Why did it start in Italy? Why did it happen at all? Many different things helped the Renaissance to happen, but it would not have happened without rich and powerful people.

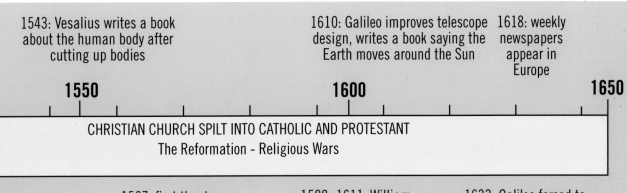

1543: Vesalius writes a book about the human body after cutting up bodies

1610: Galileo improves telescope design, writes a book saying the Earth moves around the Sun

1618: weekly newspapers appear in Europe

1550   1600   1650

CHRISTIAN CHURCH SPILT INTO CATHOLIC AND PROTESTANT
The Reformation - Religious Wars

1567: first theater built in London

1588–1611: William Shakespeare writes most of his plays

1633: Galileo forced to deny the Earth moves around the Sun

City-States

This is the city of Florence, Italy, in about 1500. The land outside the city walls was part of the city-state, but the city itself was walled in case of attack.

At the time of the Renaissance, Italy was not a single country. It was divided into many small regions, or **city-states**. A city-state was made up of a city and the land around it. The rich and powerful people who made the Renaissance possible were the rulers of the Italian city-states.

The biggest city-states, such as Venice, Genoa, and Florence, were very rich and powerful. The **dukes** who ruled them spent a lot of time trying to get more land from their neighbors. Often they would fight to get control of more land.

Sometimes the rulers of the city-states would marry into each others' families to form alliances against others.

How did the city-states become rich? Ports such as Venice and Genoa made money by **trading** silks and spices. Inland towns, such as Florence, traded too. Florence made most of its money by banking. It lent money to kings and to courts all over Europe, often to pay for wars. The wealthiest banking family, the Medici family, eventually ruled Florence.

The richest families in the city-states showed off their wealth through their clothes, homes, and posessions. They paid artists and sculptors large amounts of money to decorate the local church or cathedral. The families wanted to look wealthier than other families, and they wanted their city to look more elegant than other cities.

Benozzo Gozzoli's painting, *The Journey of the Magi*, shows part of the *Bible* story, but the painter shows the clothes and scenery of Renaissance Italy. It was painted for Lorenzo de Medici. He was the ruler of the city-state of Florence. Lorenzo is shown as the man on the white horse.

Religion

This picture shows the Holy Family, so it appears to be about religion. However, it was painted to show the importance of the family for whom it was painted. The family is shown coming down the hill. Much Renaissance art used religious themes but showed the power of the **patron** who paid for it.

At the beginning of the Renaissance, most of Europe was Christian. All of Western Europe was Catholic—they accepted the **Pope** in Rome as their leader on Earth. At that time, many important jobs in the Church were given to people because they had money and power, not always because they were religious. The Catholic Church was rich and powerful, and owned lots of land.

Religion was an important part of everyone's life. Most Renaissance paintings are Christian: they show images and stories from the *Bible*. The Church could afford to build very elegant and impressive churches.

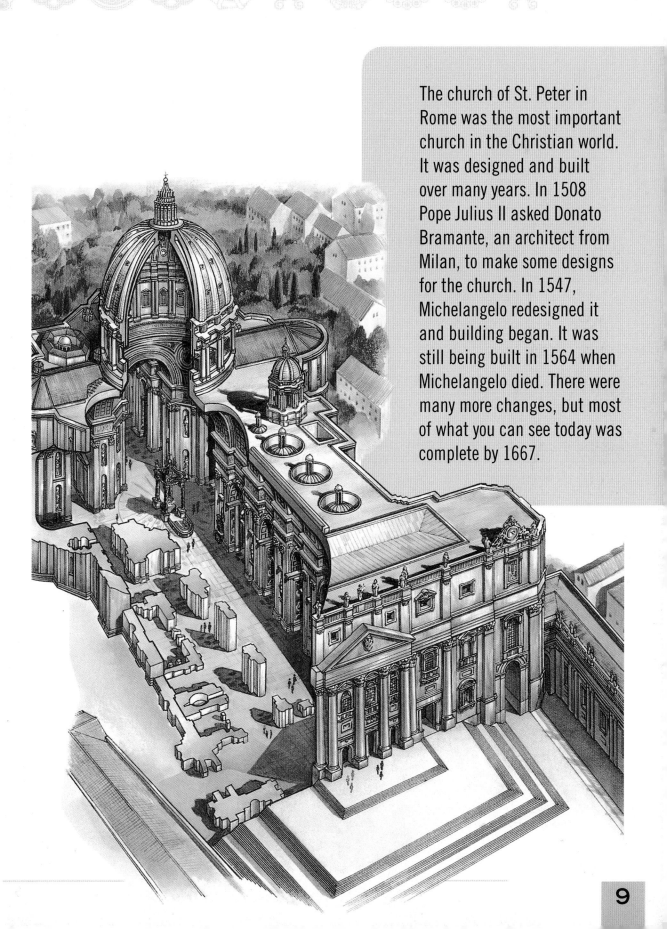

The church of St. Peter in Rome was the most important church in the Christian world. It was designed and built over many years. In 1508 Pope Julius II asked Donato Bramante, an architect from Milan, to make some designs for the church. In 1547, Michelangelo redesigned it and building began. It was still being built in 1564 when Michelangelo died. There were many more changes, but most of what you can see today was complete by 1667.

Printing

This is a page from the Gutenberg *Bible*. It has printed text and hand-illustrated borders.

Without printing, Renaissance ideas would not have spread so quickly. **Printing presses** used movable metal letters. Before printing presses were invented, each book was copied by hand or printed from carved wooden blocks. But with the printing press, many copies of a book could be printed, one after the other. The first book printed this way was the *Bible*, printed by Johannes Gutenberg in 1455.

Books and **pamphlets** could be printed quickly and cheaply. However, there were still many expensive books that were first printed on a press and then illustrated by hand.

A Printing House

Metal was melted and then poured into molds to make letters.

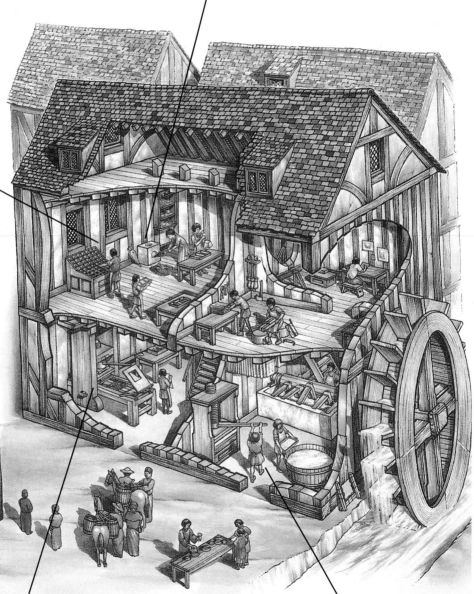

The metal letters were taken from their storage bins and made into words and sentences in wooden frames. The words had to be set backward, as they would look if held up to a mirror.

The blocks of type were put on the press and covered in ink. Paper was then pressed onto the inked letters. The reversed-type words look correct on the printed page.

Paper was made from old rags, which were made into pulp, placed in a frame, and then pressed and dried into sheets.

Trade

Marco Polo explored Asia in about 1300. He made trade contacts for Venice that made this city very rich. This picture, from a book printed in about 1400, is about his travels.

Trade made countries rich. Several **city-states**, especially Venice and Genoa, became very rich because they were the first to trade with far-off countries, such as China. They often made trade deals to be the only Europeans to buy certain **goods** from these countries. This meant they could charge other European countries very high prices for these goods.

Much trading was done by sea. Advances in ship design and **navigation** equipment allowed people to explore farther and farther as they looked for new trade routes.

Although trade made money, it was risky to be a **merchant**. Sea travel had its dangers. Pirates and bad weather could mean the loss of an expensive ship and all its cargo. There were many land routes across Europe and Asia, but land travel was difficult. Unpaved roads were dusty in summer and muddy in winter. Bandits waited along trade routes. They knew that expensive goods would travel that way.

Often, merchants from city-states such as Florence or Genoa would live for some years in other countries. Sometimes there would be a group of Italians living in a large city such as London or Paris.

Camels set off from China along the Silk Road, an old trade route. Sometimes it would take weeks to carry things to the nearest port, where the merchant's ship would be waiting.

Beauty and More

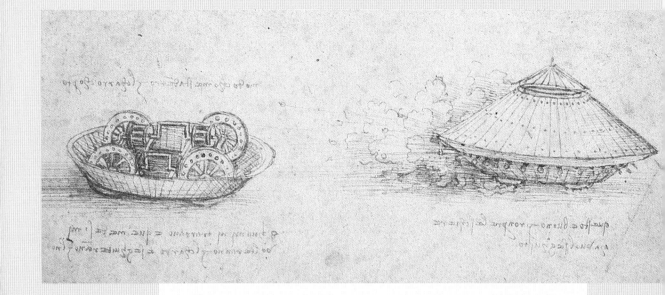

Leonardo da Vinci designed a simple tank. He was paid to design war machines such as cannons and guns for his rich patrons.

During the Renaissance, people believed that the most beautiful art was the art of ancient Greece and Rome. Artists tried to model their work on what they thought the ancient Romans would have built or painted.

Most art was paid for by **patrons**. Patrons were wealthy people who paid artists to design a house or to paint a picture.

Michelangelo was a painter, sculptor, architect, and poet. Leonardo da Vinci was a painter and a tireless inventor of gadgets and machines. The phrase "Renaissance person" is still used to describe someone who has skills and knowledge in many different subjects.

The Renaissance affected most of Europe. Many Italian artists were invited to work in other countries. Local artists then copied the new style, although sometimes they didn't understand it well.

Sometimes new ideas worked in reverse. The Dutch invented a new technique of painting, with oil paints, and the Italians learned the new method very quickly. In London, people were interested in going to the theater, often to see historical plays set in ancient Greece or Rome, or set in Renaissance Italian cities, such as Venice or Milan.

This is a modern artist's drawing of a performance of *Julius Caesar* by William Shakespeare. He was a Renaissance playwright at the Globe Theater in London, England.

Building

The beautiful stone buildings of the Renaissance were built with only very simple lifting tools and wooden scaffolding.

During the Renaissance, architects studied and copied ancient Greek and Roman architecture. They became less concerned with covering buildings with complex decoration and more concerned with relating all the parts of a building to each other mathematically. The architects used ancient ideas about **proportion**. To them, beautiful buildings were **symmetrical** and graceful. They designed buildings with round columns, curving arches, and rounded **domes**.

The dome of Florence Cathedral was designed by Filippo Brunelleschi after he studied ancient Roman buildings. Although work had started on the Cathedral many years before, nobody knew how to build such a large dome until Brunelleschi invented a new technique to complete it.

Gracious Living

Ludovico Gonzaga II, his wife Barbara (seated), their children, members of their court, and their dog, Rubino, are portrayed on one of the walls of their *palazzo*.

In Italy, the grand houses were called *palazzi*. Usually they had a courtyard in the center. The best rooms were on the second floor, where the family would meet visitors.

Many of the **courtiers** were young men who carried weapons. It was almost like a private army. Fighting often broke out between rival families. Wealthy families married their children to the children of other wealthy families to form useful alliances. The marriages were often agreed to when the children were just babies. Sometimes young girls were married to much older men whose earlier wives had died.

An Italian *Palazzo*

A private, walled garden was at the back of the house.

The courtyard did not have a roof. Some courtyards had flowers and shrubs. Others were paved.

The tall, well-lit rooms on the second floor were lived in by the family.

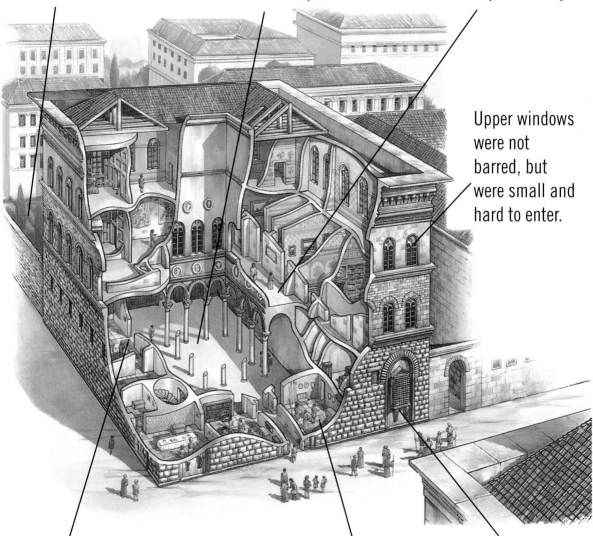

Upper windows were not barred, but were small and hard to enter.

The guardroom and office were off the main corridor. The door at the end led to the rest of the *palazzo* to make it even more secure. Only the family and their servants and guests could go beyond this door.

The lower rooms under the roof, which were hot in summer and cold in winter, were for servants and sometimes for the children of the family.

First floor windows had heavy iron bars and strong stone walls. The thick wooden door had a peephole for viewing visitors. It was protected by an iron grill.

Education

Many wealthy parents did not send their children to school. The children were taught at home by private teachers.

During the Renaissance people began to think that learning was important. The invention of the printing press made books and **pamphlets** more available. So more people began to learn to read and write.

Important people were expected to speak, read, and write several languages. They needed to know both the language of their country and Latin. They also had to know math and sciences and be skilled in hunting. Children of important people, especially boys, needed to read the latest poetry, plays, and books. Children's books told how to be a **courtier**, how to govern a country, and how to fight a successful war.

The children of less wealthy parents were expected to have some education. Even those who had to work for a living needed to be able to read, write, and have some math skills. **Merchants**, shopkeepers, and builders all needed these skills.

Girls did not need as much education as boys. Girls from wealthy families needed to read, write, and add and subtract well enough to run a household. They also had to sing, play an instrument, sew, and dance. Most girls from less important families either married or worked as household servants. They did not need an education at all.

Many children were sent to live with a master to learn a trade. At first they did the boring jobs. The man on the right is grinding ingredients for medicines.

Ordinary People

More people could read and write during the Renaissance than ever before. Many wealthy or artistic people were exploring the ideas brought up during the Renaissance. However, many workers in towns and in the country were untouched by the Renaissance. They had neither the time nor the money to explore these new ideas. They farmed the land or learned a trade such as baking, ironwork, or shoemaking. They could carry out these trades in the cities, where there were plenty of customers.

Craftworkers in towns and cities made beautiful things. This jewelry would have cost several years' wages.

Ordinary people did not live in grand homes. In towns, they lived in the poorer areas in houses close together. Often, several families shared one house. They might only have a shared yard in which to keep a few hens.

In the country, people had more space. They lived in cottages with one or two rooms. They sometimes shared the rooms with their animals by blocking off one end for them. They often had a garden for growing fruit and vegetables.

These calendar pictures show the different jobs of the farming year. The whole family worked on the land.

Food

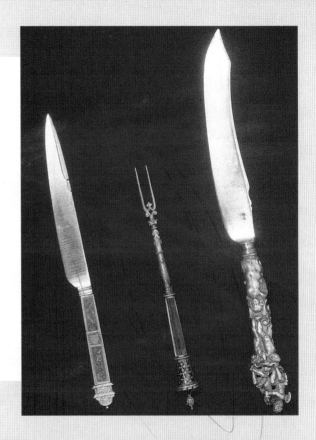

During the Renaissance, people began to use forks, as well as knives and spoons. They took these eating tools with them when they went out to eat.

Wealthy people ate a wider variety of foods during the Renaissance than ever before, thanks to the opening of **trade** routes. They ate many different kinds of wild and farmed meat and fish. They flavored meat and sweet dishes with expensive sugar, spices, and peppercorns, as well as the more ordinary honey, herbs, and flavorings. They usually drank wine.

The development of chimneys made indoor fires much safer. The kitchen developed as part of the house rather than being a separate building nearby. Large fireplaces with chimneys gave cooks a wider range of cooking equipment for roasting, boiling, and baking. Foods for feasts became more complicated.

Poor people ate cheese and bread made from coarse, dark flour. They drank milk, water, or weak beer that they brewed themselves. People who lived in the country kept chickens for eggs and sometimes a pig for meat. They ate vegetables that they grew themselves. Their homes were small, so they were likely to have just one fire for heating the room and for cooking. Sometimes they had a chimney, but more often they did not.

The people at the back are making butter from milk in the wooden barrel. The big pot on the fire was used to boil stews, oatmeal, and laundry.

Clothes

Wealthy and important people wore clothes and jewelry that showed their wealth and importance. They wore velvets, silk, fine linen cloth, and furs. They wore leather boots and shoes, and some people had indoor shoes made from expensive fabrics. There were laws in many European countries that said which fabrics, furs, and colors important people could wear. People could tell a stranger's importance by looking at his or her clothes.

Servants of wealthy people were often better dressed than many ordinary people with more important jobs. This was because a well-dressed servant showed off the master's wealth. This was especially true in Italy, where a servant's uniform told for whom he or she worked.

This painting of a wedding feast by Botticelli shows the guests and the servants in their best clothes. The guests are wearing silks, velvets, and furs. The servants are wearing brightly-colored uniforms.

A **merchant's** wife, carrying a pet dog, gives instructions to the gardener. He is taking off his hat to show respect. The lady and her husband, who is giving orders outside the garden, were allowed to wear rabbit fur. Their servants were not.

People who were not rich mostly wore clothes made from woolen cloth. Wool, and the cloth made from it, did not have to be brought to Europe from another country, so it was cheaper. Laws allowed wealthier people to wear rabbit fur on their clothes and simple jewelry. Shoes and boots were made of leather.

Most ordinary people had very few clothes. They wore their clothes for many years and mended them when necessary.

Investigating Everything

Astronomers studied the sky and made careful measurements before they drew charts of the sky. They did not just copy earlier charts.

The Renaissance was a time when people were interested in discovering things. They rediscovered the ideas of the ancient Greeks and Romans. They discovered new ideas, new countries, and how things worked.

People began to examine things carefully. They wanted to investigate and to think for themselves. They did not want to copy earlier ideas, books, and charts. People were helped in these discoveries by new inventions, such as the telescope and new **navigational** instruments.

The urge to think and investigate rather than follow old ideas began to cause problems for the church and rulers. For instance, a doctor named Vesalius said people needed to cut up human bodies to understand how they worked, rather than using animals to guess what people were like inside. Cutting up the human body was outlawed by the Christian Church. Vesalius broke the law to practice his idea.

Astronomers studied the night sky. They discovered that the Sun was at the center of the universe, while the Church said that the Earth was the center. The Church was not happy with these new ideas.

The left drawing shows what people thought a skeleton was like at the beginning of the Renaissance. The right drawing shows what Vesalius said one looked like after he cut up bodies to make careful drawings.

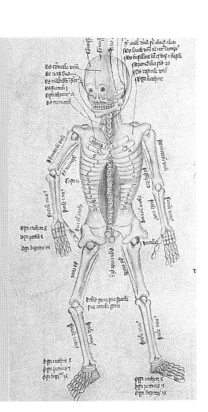
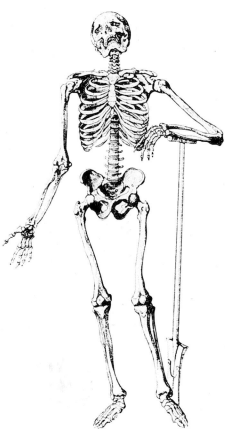

Dangerous Thinking

The Renaissance did not end at any one point in time, but between 1500 and 1600 it overlapped with an enormous change in religion—the Reformation. This started in Germany and in the Netherlands, but affected all European countries. In Germany Martin Luther had been a monk, but then left his monastery, complaining that many church leaders were more concerned with money and power than with religion. He saw no reason why priests should not marry and have children. His writings split the Church into two groups: Catholic and Protestant. This led to over 100 years of war between Christians.

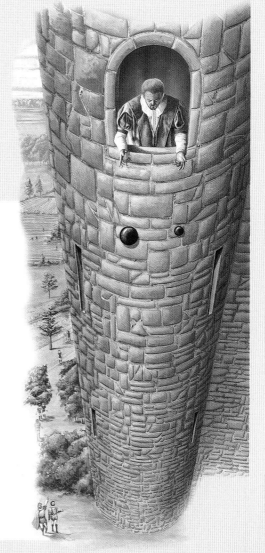

Galileo, shown here demonstrating how gravity works, made many important scientific discoveries. He showed that the Earth moves around the Sun. When he said this, the Church forced him to sign a paper saying he agreed with the Church's teaching.

Glossary

city-state   city and the towns, villages, and land around it that are controlled by the ruler of the city

courtier   person who is part of a ruler's court, who lives with the ruler and depends on him for a living

dome   curved roof covering a building

duke   ruler of an area of land called a duchy. Many city-states were ruled by dukes

goods   things made or grown to sell

merchant   person who buys things from one person and sells them to others

navigation   way of determining where you are and how to get somewhere else

pamphlet   booklet of a few printed sheets, folded together

patron   someone who regularly helps another person by giving them work or money

Pope   leader of the Catholic Church whom Christians in all countries had to obey, even before obeying their ruler

printing press   machine for books or pamphlets

proportion   pleasing or proper arrangement or balance of parts of an object

symmetrical   matching patterns on opposite sides of a dividing line or middle point

trade   buying goods in one place and taking them somewhere else to sell

Find Out More

Book to read
DK Eyewitness Books: Renaissance, Alison Cole (Dorling Kindersley, 2000)

Using the Internet
Explore the Internet to find out more about the Renaissance. Use a search engine, such as www.yahooligans.com or www.internet4kids.com and type in a keyword or phrase such as "printing press" or "Vesalius".

Index